Robert Jager

Aphorisms
for Clarinet and Piano

ISBN 978-1-4234-8303-8

EDWARD B. MARKS MUSIC COMPANY / EXCLUSIVELY DISTRIBUTED BY HAL•LEONARD® CORPORATION

7777 W. BLUEMOUND RD. P.O. BOX 13819 MILWAUKEE, WI 53213

www.ebmarks.com
www.halleonard.com

Aphorisms
for Clarinet and Piano

Robert Jager

- I -

Pensively ($\bullet$ = ca.64)

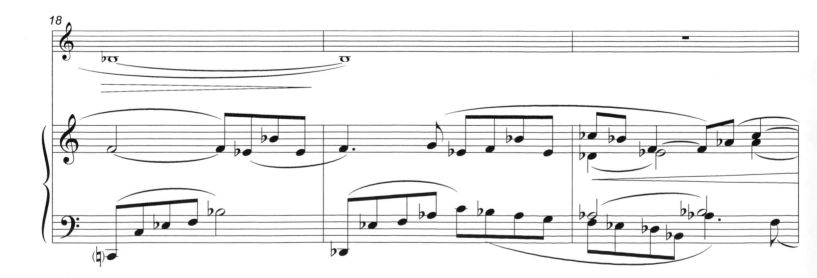

Lightly, Dance-like (♩= *ca.*84)

rit.　　　　　　Pensively ($\bullet$= *ca.*64)

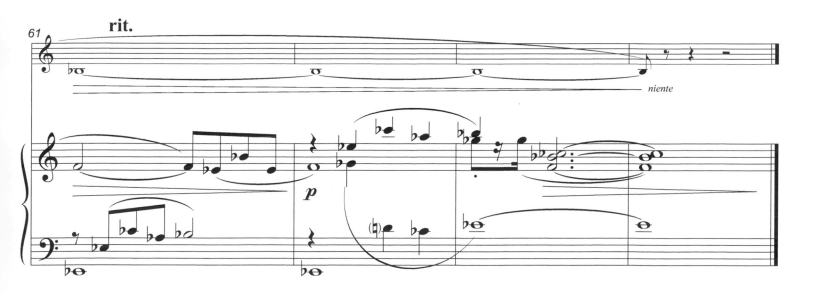

- II -

Liltingly (♩. = *ca.*68)

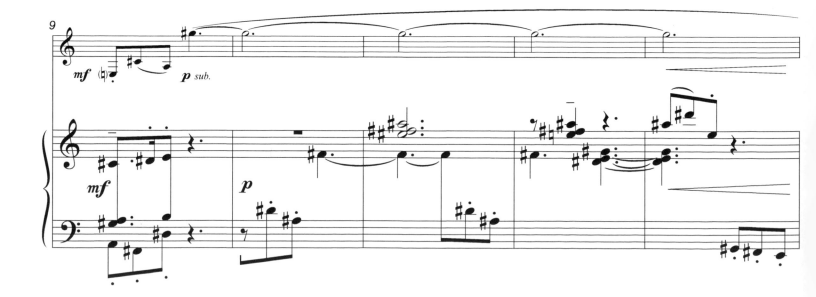

Robert Jager

Aphorisms
for Clarinet and Piano

ISBN 978-1-4234-8303-8

EDWARD B. MARKS MUSIC COMPANY / EXCLUSIVELY DISTRIBUTED BY HAL•LEONARD® CORPORATION

7777 W. BLUEMOUND RD. P.O. BOX 13819 MILWAUKEE, WI 53213

www.ebmarks.com
www.halleonard.com

for Garry Evans

Aphorisms
for Clarinet and Piano

Robert Jager

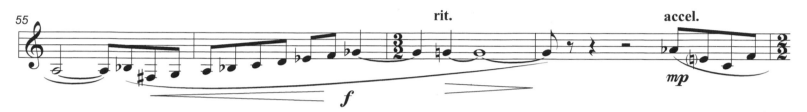

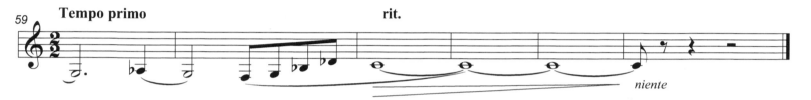

II

Liltingly (♩.= ca.68)

4

III

Furiously ($\quad$ = *ca.*112)

IV

Very Slow and Reflective ($\quad$ = *ca.*36)

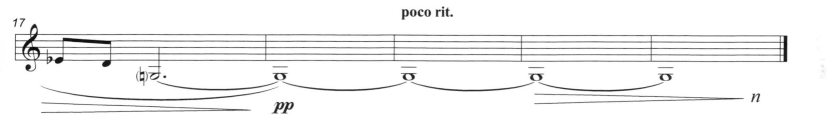

poco rit.

V. Smithville/July

Boisterously ($\quad$= *ca.*120)

BLANK FOR PAGE TURN

- III -

Furiously ($\quarternote$ = *ca.*112)

- IV -

Very Slow and Reflective (♩ = *ca.*36)

V. Smithville/July

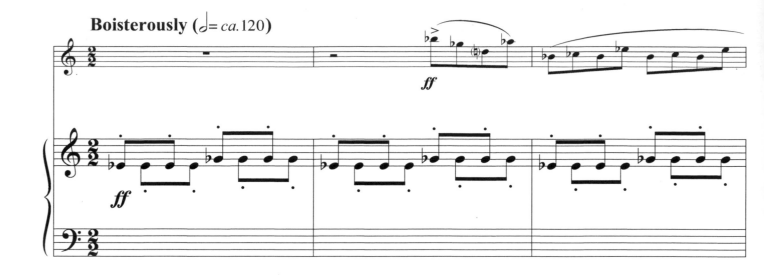

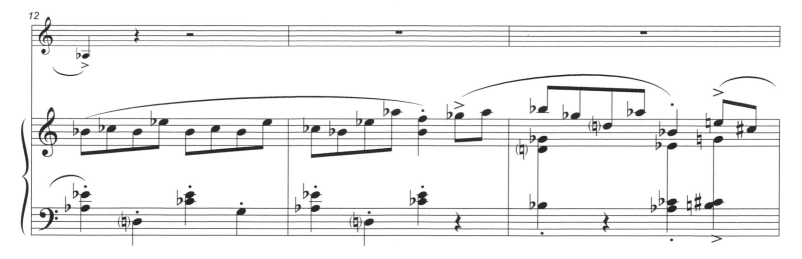